HOW TO BE A
LADYBIRD

written by **LAURA KNOWLES**

illustrated by **STEVEN WOOD**

HOW TO BE A
LADYBIRD

Hello, I'm Charles Darwing, and I'm in a garden not very far from where you're sitting now. You've arrived just in time to follow the adventures of a plucky little ladybird as she sets off on life's great journey.

FOR ANY WANNABE LADYBIRDS OUT THERE, YOU'RE ABOUT TO DISCOVER:

- WHAT TO EAT

- HOW TO TURN INTO A PUPA

- WAYS TO DEFEND YOURSELF AGAINST ENEMIES

- WHERE TO FIND A COSY SPOT FOR WINTER

If you want to spot ladybirds out in the real world, look out for my **BUG HUNTER TIPS**. They'll give you a helping hand.

Can you spot the ladybird eggs yet? You're going to have to look closer than that.

No, not there. Those are dewdrops.

Nope. Still cold. Those are flowers.

Now you're getting close. Look under those leaves.

BUG-HUNTER TIP

IF YOU'RE LUCKY ENOUGH TO SPOT A LADYBIRD LAYING HER EGGS, DON'T DISTURB HER. THE SEVEN-SPOT LADYBIRD LAYS AROUND 15-20 YELLOW EGGS, OFTEN ON THE UNDERSIDE OF A LEAF.

7

The hungry ladybird larvae will gobble up 1,500 aphids during their year-long life. Bad news for aphids, great news for gardeners.

HOW TO EAT LIKE A LADYBIRD LARVA

- DON'T WORRY ABOUT VARIETY. APHIDS ARE YOUR SUPERFOOD!

- WHEN YOU'RE NEWLY HATCHED, JUST SUCK UP THE APHIDS' JUICES.

- AS YOU GROW BIGGER, USE YOUR SHARP MOUTHPARTS TO CHOMP, CHOMP, CHOMP.

- GOBBLE THE OCCASIONAL MITE OR OTHER TINY INSECT IF THEY COME YOUR WAY.

- EAT AT LEAST 10 APHIDS EACH DAY. YOU'VE GOT A LOT OF GROWING TO DO.

Full to the brim, Dotty wanders off to explore her nettle plant. But there's danger lurking among these leaves...

I wouldn't go near – oh, too late!

Well, well, well. Who do we have here?

Hi there! I'm Dotty. I'm new around here. I like your stripes, very eye-catching!

Oops, actually, my brothers and sisters will be wondering where I am. Better be going... it was nice meeting you...

Oh, don't go yet. You look so... juicy.

Well, isn't it obvious? You're a seven-spot ladybird just like me. Or at least you will be, once you grow up a bit.

I'm going to be like you?! WOW! So, will you be my friend?

Ha, no way. I'm far too busy.

BUG-HUNTER TIP

LOOK OUT FOR LADYBIRD LARVAE IN LATE SPRING AND EARLY SUMMER. BECAUSE THEY LOOK SO UNLIKE ADULT LADYBIRDS, YOU MAY HAVE ALREADY SEEN THEM WITHOUT REALISING WHAT THEY WERE.

How am I going to change into a ladybird? I don't look anything like one! It's so confusing. Hasn't anyone written a how-to guide yet?

My skin is starting to feel reeeeally tight.

MUNCH
MUNCH
MUNCH

WIGGLE... JIGGLE... POP!

MUNCH MUNCH MUNCH

WIGGLE... JIGGLE... POP!

WIGGLE...
JIGGLE... POP!

Am I a ladybird now?!
No... still a larva.

Now I must be a ladybird! Nope. Just a bigger larva.

This time I MUST have turned into a ladybird. Oh, c'mon! I'm bored of being a larva now. I wanna be a grown-up!

HOW TO CHANGE INTO A LADYBIRD

- EAT LOTS OF APHIDS AND SHED YOUR SKIN THREE TIMES, GROWING BIGGER EACH TIME. THIS WILL TAKE THREE TO SIX WEEKS.

- STICK YOURSELF TO A LEAF AND STOP MOVING.

- SHED YOUR SKIN ONE LAST TIME TO REVEAL A HARD PUPA. STAY INSIDE FOR SEVEN TO TEN DAYS WHILE YOU REBUILD YOUR BODY.

- SQUEEZE OUT OF YOUR PUPA. TA DA!

Ahh, that was a good snooze...

Hey, you look just like me! Are your wings all soft, too?

Yeah... I just want to be able to fly!

HOW TO TURN RED

- EAT PLENTY OF SCRUMMY APHIDS WHILE YOU ARE A LARVA.

- THIS WILL HELP YOUR BODY MAKE LOTS OF THE COLOURING NEEDED TO TURN YOUR WING CASES RED.

- AFTER HATCHING FROM YOUR PUPA, WAIT FOR A FEW DAYS FOR YOUR WING CASES TO HARDEN AND CHANGE COLOUR FROM YELLOW TO RED.

- WATCH OUT FOR PREDATORS UNTIL YOU GET YOUR WARNING COLOURS. THEY WON'T KNOW THAT YOU TASTE YUCKY!

WHAT IS A LADYBIRD?

You'll have noticed by now that ladybird larvae and adults look very different from one another. Imagine looking that different from your parents! Look closely, though, and you'll notice they share some features.

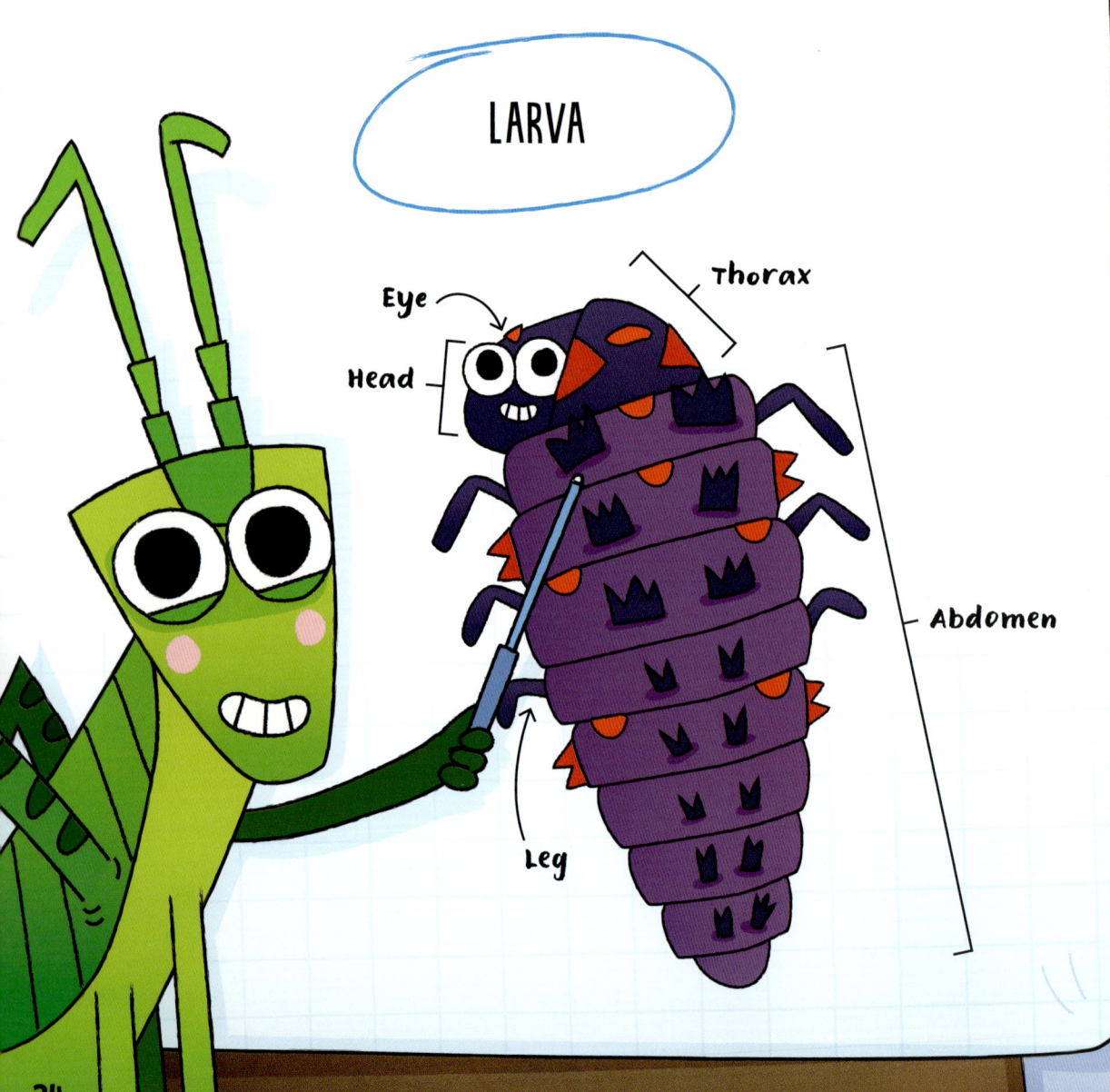

LARVA

Eye

Head

Thorax

Abdomen

Leg

ADULT LADYBIRD

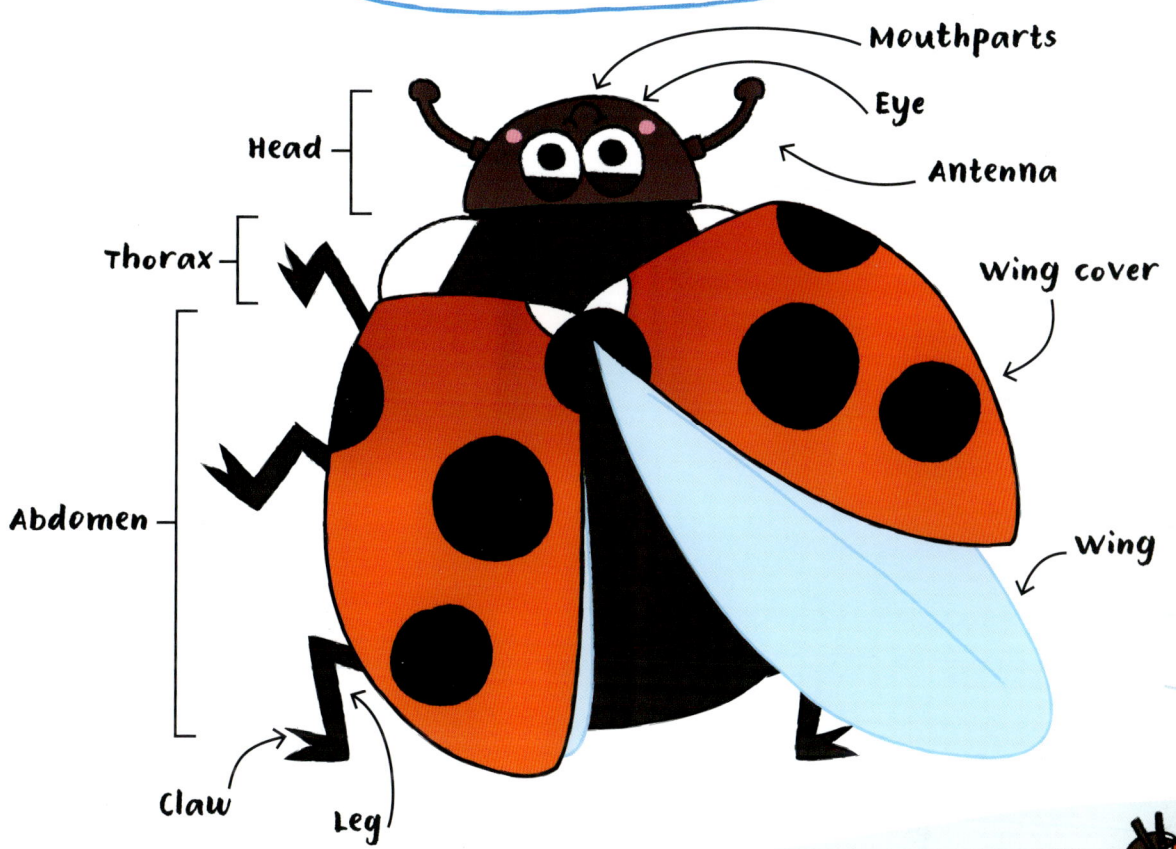

Mouthparts

Eye

Antenna

Head

Thorax

Abdomen

Wing cover

Wing

Claw

Leg

Like all insects, ladybirds have six legs and a body made of three sections – head, thorax, and abdomen.

ELYTRA

THE PROPER NAME FOR A LADYBIRD'S SPOTTY WING CASES IS 'ELYTRA' (SAY EL-I-TRA). NEXT TIME YOU SPOT A LADYBIRD, SEE IF YOU CAN IMPRESS SOMEONE WITH THIS FANCY WORD.

As our little ladybird waits for her wing cases to harden and her pattern to emerge, she lies low. This is not a time to attract attention. After a few days, her transformation is complete...

YAWN! I've been hanging about on this branch for ages. It's so BORING. I need to get some exercise.

Hang on a minute... MY WINGS ARE WORKING!

Show off.
Hey, snails! Look at meeeee! Jealous?

Snack! Snack! I see a snack!

As you have just witnessed, some birds are not put off by ladybirds' warning colours. While most animals think ladybirds taste revolting, swallows, swifts, and house martins are all happy to gulp down ladybirds without feeling poorly.

30

HOW TO FLY

- LIFT UP YOUR WING CASES (THERE'S A HINGE JUST BEHIND YOUR HEAD).

- UNFOLD YOUR DELICATE WINGS.

- BEAT YOUR WINGS VERY QUICKLY – 85 TIMES EVERY SECOND SHOULD DO THE TRICK!

Ah, this pond looks nice and calm...
Woah, didn't your mother tell you it was rude to stick out your tongue?

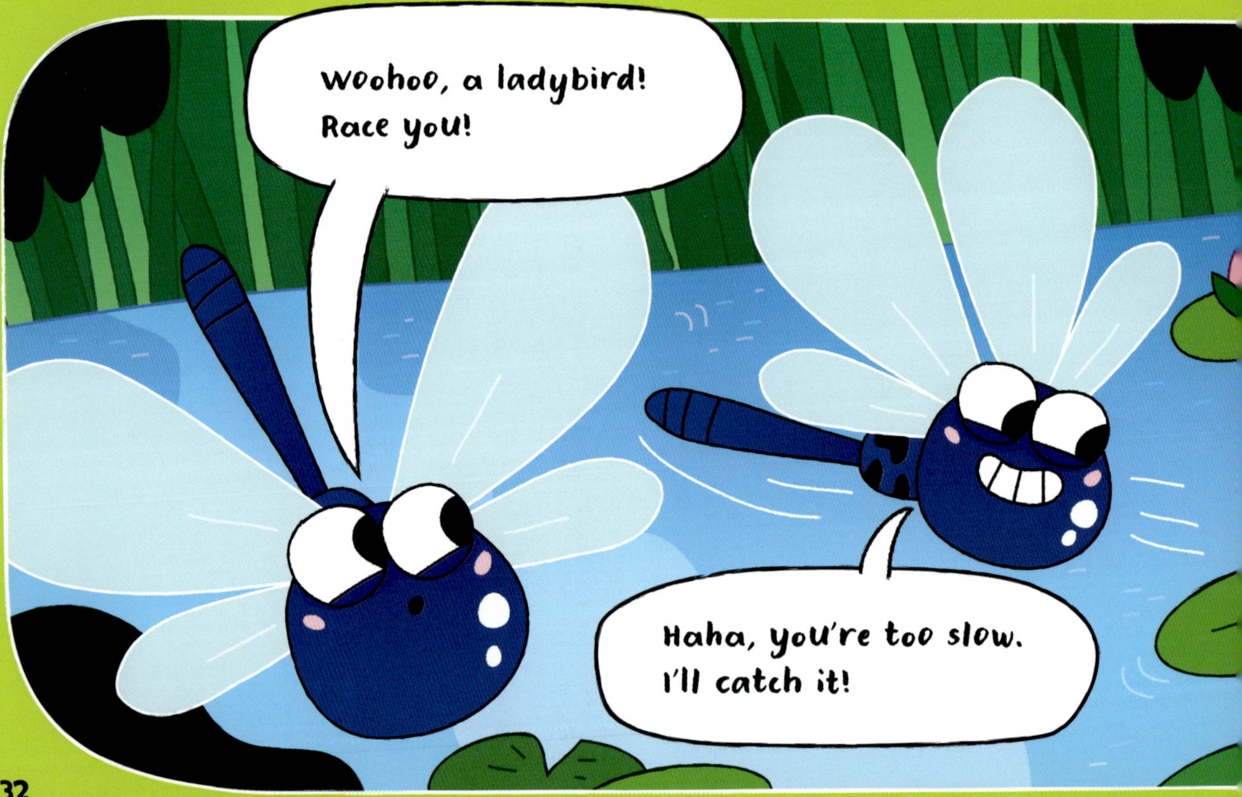
Woohoo, a ladybird! Race you!
Haha, you're too slow. I'll catch it!

33

Welcome to the Ladybird Fashion Show! From two spots to 24 spots, there is a pattern for everyone.

Next Up: Eileen the Eyed Ladybird. Tell us: where have you travelled from today, Eileen?

I've come from the pine forest!

Beautiful. Now here comes Velma, a 24-spot ladybird. Tell us a bit about yourself, Velma.

I don't like aphids! My favourite foods are red campion and false oat grass.

Did you know, some 2-spot ladybirds are black with red spots!

2-SPOT LADYBIRD

SIZE: 3-6 MM

EATS: APHIDS

HABITAT: ALL, INCLUDING GARDENS AND PARKS

7-SPOT LADYBIRD

SIZE: 6-8 MM

EATS: APHIDS

HABITAT: ALL, INCLUDING GARDENS AND PARKS

14-SPOT LADYBIRD

SIZE: 4-5 MM

EATS: APHIDS

HABITAT: ALL, INCLUDING GARDENS AND PARKS

ADONIS' LADYBIRD

SIZE: 4-5 MM

EATS: APHIDS

HABITAT: WEEDS AND WASTELAND

PINE LADYBIRD

SIZE: 3-4.5 MM

EATS: APHIDS AND SCALE INSECTS

HABITAT: PINE TREES

ORANGE LADYBIRD

SIZE: 5-6 MM

EATS: MILDEW

HABITAT: WOODLAND

ALL SORTS OF LADYBIRDS

There are more than 6,000 ladybird species around the world. Who knows - there might be a few still to be discovered!

16-SPOT LADYBIRD

SIZE: 3 MM

EATS: POLLEN, NECTAR, AND FUNGI

HABITAT: GRASSLAND

22-SPOT LADYBIRD

SIZE: 3-4 MM

EATS: MILDEW

HABITAT: GARDENS AND GRASSY PLACES

This ladybird looks velvety.

24-SPOT LADYBIRD

SIZE: 3-4 MM

EATS: RED CAMPION AND FALSE OAT GRASS

HABITAT: GRASSLAND

HARLEQUIN LADYBIRD

SIZE: 8-10 MM

EATS: APHIDS AND OTHER INSECTS INCLUDING LADYBIRD EGGS AND LARVAE

HABITAT: ALL, INCLUDING GARDENS AND PARKS

CREAM-SPOT LADYBIRD

SIZE: 4-6 MM

EATS: APHIDS

HABITAT: WOODLAND, SHRUBS, AND HEDGEROWS

EYED LADYBIRD

SIZE: 8-10 MM

EATS: APHIDS

HABITAT: PINE TREES

They can be many different colours - including red, black, yellow, cream, or even blue! Here are just a few of the six-legged beauties.

The air is growing chilly, the days are getting shorter, and there aren't enough aphids to eat. That can mean only one thing: it's time to sleep through the winter.

Hey, excuse me! It's getting cold around here! Do you know anywhere warm and safe?

You bet I do! I know the perfect old log. All my friends are going to sleep there. Follow me!

BUG-HUNTER TIP

SOME INSECTS AND OTHER ANIMALS SLOW RIGHT DOWN AND STOP MOVING AROUND DURING THE WINTER MONTHS. IF YOU DISCOVER A GROUP OF SLEEPING LADYBIRDS IN WINTER, LEAVE THEM AS YOU FOUND THEM.

HOW TO FIND YOUR FRIENDS

WHEN IT'S TIME TO SLEEP THROUGH WINTER, YOU'LL WANT TO FIND OTHER LADYBIRDS. TOGETHER, YOUR RED-AND-BLACK WARNING COLOURS OFFER EVEN BETTER PROTECTION. SNIFF OUT THE CHEMICAL SIGNALS OTHER LADYBIRDS GIVE OFF TO FIND OUT WHERE THEY'RE HIDING.

WHERE TO SLEEP IN WINTER

- CRACKS IN OLD LOGS AND TREE BARK
- IN HOLLOW PLANT STEMS
- GAPS BETWEEN ROCKS
- UNDER FALLEN LEAVES
- GARDEN SHEDS AND OTHER BUILDINGS

If you didn't know better, you might think all the ladybirds have flown off to distant lands. But no – they are hiding away, waiting for spring.

Our little ladybird is tucked up, sleeping soundly. She uses very little energy during these dark, frosty months.

zzzzzzz
zzzzzzz
zzzzzzz

After several months tucked up quiet and still, the warming weather is waking up the dozing ladybirds.

Our plucky ladybird is off to find some food. Luckily, lots of new aphids hatch out in the spring, making a perfect breakfast buffet.

Aphids... where are you, aphids? I'm coming to find yoooou....

What a beautiful day! The leaves are green, the sun is shining, the birds are cheeping. Uh oh – the birds are cheeping!

48

HOW TO STAY SAFE FROM PREDATORS

- TUCK YOUR LEGS IN UNDER YOUR BODY.

- OOZE STINKY YELLOW LIQUID OUT OF YOUR LEG JOINTS (THIS IS CALLED REFLEX BLOOD).

- WAIT FOR THE SCARY PREDATOR TO GO AWAY.

- GO BACK TO MUNCHING ON APHIDS.

LADYBIRD PREDATORS

Predators are animals that hunt and eat other animals. Even with their clever defence tactics, ladybirds still have plenty of dastardly predators.

PARASITIC WASPS AND FLIES

SOME WASPS AND FLIES LAY THEIR EGGS INSIDE LADYBIRDS. WHEN THEY HATCH, THEY EAT THE LADYBIRD FROM THE INSIDE. TALK ABOUT AN UNINVITED GUEST!

FROGS AND TOADS

THESE JUMPY CRITTERS WILL OFTEN GOBBLE LADYBIRDS. THEY SNATCH THEM WITH THEIR STICKY TONGUE BEFORE THEY EVEN KNOW WHAT IT IS THEY'RE EATING.

SPIDERS AND INSECTS

SOME SPIDERS, BEETLES, WASPS, ANTS, AND DRAGONFLIES WILL CATCH AND EAT LADYBIRDS.

BIRDS

SOME BIRDS, SUCH AS SWIFTS AND SWALLOWS, AREN'T BOTHERED BY LADYBIRDS' DEFENSIVE CHEMICALS. THE BIRDS GULP THEM DOWN AS THEY FLY THROUGH THE AIR — ALTHOUGH SOMETIMES THEY SPIT THEM OUT!

OTHER LADYBIRDS

IF THERE ISN'T MUCH FOOD ABOUT, LADYBIRDS WILL EAT OTHER LADYBIRD EGGS, LARVAE, AND PUPAE. HARLEQUINS, ORIGINALLY FROM ASIA, ARE PARTICULARLY KEEN ON A TASTY LADYBIRD SNACK.

LADYBIRD PREY

Ladybirds are famous for guzzling pesky
aphids, but there are plenty of other
mouthwatering meals on the menu.
Do any of these look tasty to you?

OTHER LADYBIRD EGGS AND LARVAE

SOME CALL IT BAD MANNERS.
LADYBIRDS CALL IT A FREE DINNER.

APHIDS

THESE TINY SAP-SUCKERS ARE
LADYBIRDS' FAVOURITE FOOD.

MITES AND MEALYBUGS

MOST LADYBIRDS WON'T TURN
THEIR NOSES UP AT THESE MICRO
MINIBEASTS. IN FACT, ALMOST ANY
TINY, SOFT INSECT WILL MAKE A
YUMMY LADYBIRD LUNCH.

MILDEW
A FEW TYPES OF LADYBIRD ARE VEGETARIAN. THEY EAT PLANTS, MILDEW, AND MOULDS INSTEAD OF OTHER INSECTS.

INSECT EGGS
THESE CAN'T CRAWL AWAY, SO THEY ARE EASY PICKINGS!

POLLEN AND NECTAR
THIS FLORAL FOOD SOUNDS A LOT TASTIER THAN MOULD! ALL ADULT LADYBIRDS SNACK ON THESE SWEET TREATS IN EARLY SPRING, WHEN THERE AREN'T MANY APHIDS ABOUT.

Right, pull yourself together, Dotty. You've been asleep for months and you need to find some aphids. Now, where could they be hiding....

Ugh, concrete. There won't be any here.

Maybe I'll find a few snacks in the nice green grass...

Hey, this isn't grass! It's horrible spiky plastic! And it's HOT!

OUCH!

Quick, I've gotta get out of here.

Aha, that flowery shrub looks good. There must be some food for me there.

Yeeeuck! What's it been covered in?!

COUGH SPLUTTER CHOKE

Whatever it is, it can't be good. There are no other bugs ANYWHERE!

BUG-HUNTER TIP

TO ENCOURAGE LADYBIRDS AND OTHER INSFCTS TO VISIT YOUR GARDEN, CHOOSE REAL GRASS INSTEAD OF ARTIFICIAL GRASS AND DON'T SPRAY PESTICIDES – IT WILL KILL THE INSECTS.

What am I going to do? Where am I going to go? Is nowhere safe?

Hey, what's the trouble? Anything I can do to help?

I've just woken up from my winter sleep and I'm so hungry, but I can't find anywhere safe to land! I can't find any aphids!

Oh dear, that does sound difficult. Well, I sometimes see them when I'm drinking nectar from flowers. Let me think... there are some lovely plants along by the railway track.

58

HOW TO HELP LADYBIRDS

Would you like to make your garden or balcony an inviting place for ladybirds to live or visit? Here are some simple things you can do to be a friend to these cute and colourful insects.

BUILD A BUG HOTEL

Ask your grown-up to build a bug hotel. Some old wood, pieces of bamboo cane, pine cones, leaves, and a roof of old tiles or short planks of wood will give ladybirds a warm place to spend the winter. Ladybirds also hunker down in hollow stems, so tell your grown-ups not to cut back old plant stems until spring.

DON'T USE PESTICIDES

Encourage your grown-ups not to spray pesticides on their plants. These will kill the aphids that the ladybirds eat, as well as any ladybirds that are on the plants.

GARDENERS LOVE LADYBIRDS BECAUSE THEY EAT THE PESTS THAT DAMAGE FRUIT, VEGETABLES, AND FLOWERS.

GIVE THEM DRINKING WATER

Leave a shallow dish of water out so that ladybirds - and other insects and birds - have somewhere to drink when the weather is dry.

GLOSSARY

Dotty's world contains words you might not have come across before. Here you'll find the meanings of some important words to know when learning about ladybirds.

APHID

Sap-sucking bug that is a favourite food of many ladybirds

INSECT

Animal with six legs and a three part-body

LARVA

Stage of a ladybird's life after it hatches from an egg and before it becomes a pupa

MOULTING

When a larva sheds its skin

PESTICIDE

Chemical that kills pest insects, but can also harm other insects, such as ladybirds

PREY

Animal that is eaten
by other animals

PREDATOR

Animal that eats
other animals

REFLEX BLOOD

Liquid produced by
ladybirds that puts off
predators because of
its smell and taste

PUPA

Stage of a ladybird's
life before it becomes
an adult

WARNING COLOUR

Animal colour that warns
predators it tastes unpleasant
or could be harmful to eat

WING CASE

Hard wing that protects
the more delicate
membranous wing

DK | Penguin Random House

Author Laura Knowles
Illustrator Steven Wood

Project Editor Kathleen Teece
Project Art Editor Polly Appleton
Managing Editor Gemma Farr
Managing Art Editor Anna Hall
Production Editor Gillian Reid
Production Controller Magdalena Bojko
Jacket Designer Polly Appleton

Consultant Prof. Helen Roy, Ecologist at the
UK Centre for Ecology & Hydrology and
Professor of Ecology at the University of Exeter

Royal Entomological Society

Director of Publishing Emilie Aimé
Outreach and Engagement Officer Francisca Sconce

Royal Entomological Society – enrich the world
with insect science **www.royensoc.co.uk**

First published in Great Britain in 2025 by
Dorling Kindersley Limited
20 Vauxhall Bridge Road,
London SW1V 2SA
In association with the Royal Entomological Society

The authorised representative in the EEA is
Dorling Kindersley Verlag GmbH. Arnulfstr. 124,
80636 Munich, Germany

A CIP catalogue record for this book
is available from the British Library.
ISBN: 978-0-2416-8585-3

Printed and bound in China

www.dk.com

This book was made with Forest
Stewardship Council™ certified
paper – one small step in DK's
commitment to a sustainable future.
Learn more at www.dk.com/uk/
information/sustainability

MIX
Paper | Supporting
responsible forestry
FSC™ C018179